Pip!

Written by Suzannah Ditchburn
Illustrated by Estelle Corke

Collins

Sam pats Pip.

Dad pats Pip.

pat

Tip it in.

tin

4

Pip tip tips it.

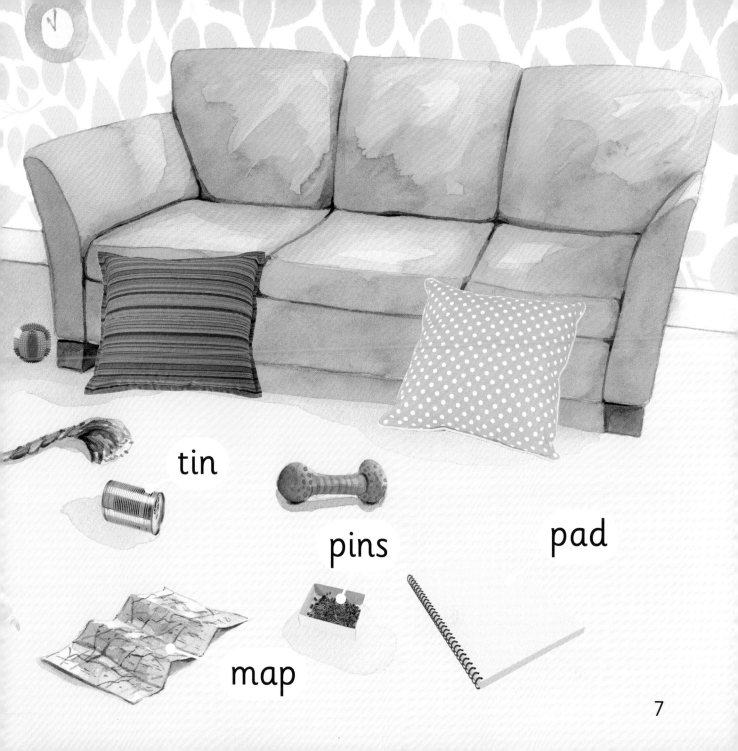

tin

pins

pad

map

Pip sits.

pat pat

8

9

Pip dips. Pip tips.

Sam sips. Dad sips.

Pip naps.

Dad naps. Sam naps.

/m/

14

/d/

15

🐾 Review: After reading 🐾

Use your assessment from hearing the children read to choose any GPCs, words or tricky words that need additional practice.

Read 1: Decoding

- Turn to pages 6 and 7. Ask the children to find, point to and read words that end with the sound /p/. (*Pip, tip, map*)
- Repeat for:

  /s/   (*tips, pins*) (t/i/p/s, p/i/n/s)

  /n/   (*tin*)   (t/i/n)

- Look at the "I spy sounds" pages (14–15) together. How many objects can the children point out that contain the /m/ sound and the /d/ sound? (e.g. *map, pram, man, magazine, money; dog, beard, doll, dinosaur*)

Read 2: Prosody

- Model reading each page with expression to the children. After you have read each page, ask the children to have a go at reading with expression.
- On pages 4 and 5 show the children how you point to objects when you read the label and use a child's voice for the words in the speech bubble and the sound words.

Read 3: Comprehension

- For every question ask the children how they know the answer. Ask:
  - Who is Pip? (*the dog*)
  - Who is Sam? (*the boy*)
  - What does Pip tip over? (*the table*)
  - Where do you think Dad and Sam took Pip to play outside (pages 10–11)? (*the park*)
  - What have you learnt about looking after a pet dog from reading this book? (e.g. *it sips drink from a bowl, it likes to make a mess*)